SECOND-YEAR

Widow

The Path From Grief to
Transformation

ANNE THROWER

This book is dedicated to the many widows who are on their own grief path.

ACKNOWLEDGMENTS

N o one should go through grief alone. Even those of us who think we are too independent should call on others during a loss. I think the same holds true for putting together a book on grief.

I relied a lot on experts in the field—many who have written wonderful books—during the grieving process and while writing this book. They were gracious to give me permission to acknowledge their work in my book and to formally recognize them in the book. I did pass around a rough draft of my book for people to read. Miriam Krasno, a good friend who just happens to be a good editor, was one of the early readers of the book. Her insights were invaluable as were Dr. Muriel Fuqua, English professor in the School of Humanities and Communication at Daytona State College. Dr. Fuqua's background in theology and experience as a self-published author was literally a God-send for me. Mac's cousin, Marie, was also gracious enough to look through a rough copy.

I thought it would be important to ask a couple of widow friends to look at the book from a widow's perspective. Susan Casper, who volunteers with me at a local hospice, and Anne Nussle, whom I know through church, were kind enough to look over my copy. And my dear friends, Cathy Rinehart and Ann Hauptman, were also invaluable during the writing process.

But it's with humility I want to thank you, the reader, for taking the chance to see if this book and its unknown author may have something that will help your journey. I hope I didn't disappoint. Another good friend, Todd Richardson, picked up my book proofs one night and without prompting read the entire book and gently offered suggestions. I had been thinking of asking him, but I didn't want him to feel obligated. We all need friends like that.

And, finally, I would like to thank Mac for his guidance. He was there in spirit, and I would like to believe, smiling, as I worked on this book.

CHAPTER 1.

A Year Later

> "Whenever I find myself growing grim about the mouth;
> whenever it is a damp, drizzly November in my soul…I
> account it high time to get to the sea as soon as I can."
> —<u>Herman Melville</u>, *Moby-Dick*

On the morning of the one-year anniversary of Mac's death, I found myself at his parents' grave in a small, rural North Carolina town. While Mac had never lived in the town, I thought it was important to bring a part of him home, especially to his mom, Isabella, whom he adored. His only brother had agreed. So, my brother-in-law, George, his wife, Deborah, and I had decided to set off for Red Springs. The previous day, I had ridden a train with Mac's ashes through the North Carolina countryside to the Charlotte area where Mac grew up.

When we arrived at the gravesite, we saw a small, pink artificial rose imbedded in the ground near his mother's grave. We were struck by its simplicity and symbolism. Pink roses—not to mention my pink wedding dress—were an important part of our mountain wedding twenty-three years earlier. We stood in silence as Mac's ashes were spread, and then all three of us embraced. It was beautiful.

In rural North Carolina, the day after Thanksgiving doesn't have the big city bustle that major cities have. We did, however, manage to find a Christian bookstore that doubled as a florist. Among the displays was a perfect artificial pink rose arrangement inside a spiked pink cone. So we returned to the cemetery where George placed the flowers at the Thrower headstone.

Mac died of a massive heart attack on Thanksgiving morning, November 28, 2013. He was home in bed when I heard him scream. I knew immediately what was going on since he had been living with an artificial valve for fourteen years. I ran from the living room and called 911. I never heard Mac's voice again.

So my grief journey began. The first year now seems like a blur. Many people and books helped me through that first year. But the second year was different.

I remember waking up the morning of the first-year anniversary of Mac's death thinking what a year it had been: Mac's death, losing my job, a minor car wreck, selling our dream home, and downsizing to something more affordable. It had all seemed to work out—with God's help—including a new job at the same college where I had been laid off. The almost three months I was without a job were the perfect foundation for examining the rest of my life. It gave me time to think.

I, like many people who have lost a loved one, thought the first year would be the hardest, and then life would begin to get back to normal. I envisioned the second year as being all about moving from the past to the present and finding a new purpose in life. In some ways, that is what happened. However, I really wasn't ready for some unexpected bumps along the road.

I had learned the second year for me was also hard. While the first year was all about adrenaline, the second year was more complex. There were so many things going through my head, ideas I never would have explored if Mac were still alive. I spent hours thinking of all the things I still wanted to accomplish. But I wanted to be prepared if I died suddenly at fifty-nine, even though I had no health problems that indicated that could happen.

Regardless of those pesky worries, I was ready now to explore my second year without Mac. While even today, I still don't know exactly what all will happen to me, I'm more settled, calm and comfortable about the future. It was during the second year when I truly realized you can't rush grief. Like waiting out a storm, there is no quick way to get around it. I was accepting that I just had to experience it for as long as it takes.

Even with grieving, I'm still planning the future, and I'm not as lost. I have added some direction to my life. And probably most importantly, I have had the opportunity to pause and look at life anew. I want to value the solid relationships that I now have and continue to enjoy the experiences living in the here and now. But most of all, I want to remember and continue to find ways to integrate Mac into my life forever.

I'm not one to dwell on the past. However, my experience as a widow may prove helpful to others who are learning to craft a new life without their spouses. I offer my insight and some practical advice with the hope that it will ease the journey for others.

Lagniappe is an old New Orleans Creole word meaning "something extra." I hope this book will be *lagniappe* for my widow companions.

CHAPTER 2.

Listening to God

"Where there is strife, there is pride, but wisdom is found in
those who take advice."
—Proverbs 13:10 (NIV)

The second year took on new meaning about who I was and what I
hoped to achieve, while the first year was about getting through the
loss of Mac, a process that at times was numbing. I never questioned why
God allowed Mac to die when he did. I always believed this was part of God's
greater plan. But I already had a connection with God in the months leading
up to his death. I was a regular churchgoer, but only recently.

From the day Mac died, I started to listen to God; however, during the
second year, there were times His direction intensified and seemed even more
important. I began to understand that there were lessons to be learned from
Mac's death. And during that process, I started to see other benefits from the
mourning. But it wasn't always a natural progression.

At times, I thought I was like the person who was yelling and strug-
gling just to make it through the day. While other times, I would wake up
calm, knowing that God had a part of giving me that peaceful time. There
was never a specific reason why or when the calm would come. But it was

comforting, and often those mornings offered direction. I learned that what I really needed to do was to calm down long enough to listen to what God was saying and to connect the dots. I also learned to accept that there would be times that I would not understand God's timing or His purpose, but that He was doing what was best for me. He was taking me on a new journey, and the seed had been planted.

It was well into the second year—after a lot of reading of the Bible and books on grieving —that I began to understand and accept that God was building on some of my strengths such as my resilience and ability to accept change. I had read that one of the "benefits" from mourning was often a deeper faith. I can say that was the case for me. I am thankful to see this so clearly in my lifetime.

At first, I thought people were just being kind to me because I was a recent widow. *They were in the right place at the right time*, I thought. Then it dawned on me that God was helping me, often working through other people. I just had to ask and pray. I started to see God as a caring friend who was compassionate and willing to listen. And I laid it all out to Him, the good and the bad, and then I let go and put it in His hands.

It was during the second year when I realized that my most important prayer to God was for awareness and the strength to put everything in His hands. I no longer prayed for specifics. Sure, I prayed to God when my doctor said I needed a CT scan to check scarring on this former smoker's lungs. But the prayer was to put the matter in His hands and not for good results. As it turned out, it was good results.

Trusting God as part of my prayers helped in other ways. I no longer blamed myself for what went wrong. I used to say: "*Mac would have lived if I had prayed more to God*," or "*If I had been a better person, God would have allowed Mac to live*." I became more comfortable with crying. I started to realize that expressing emotion with tears was a gift from God, and that God even kept track of those tears. As Psalm 56:8 (NLT) says, "You keep track of all my sorrows. You have collected all my tears in your bottle…" I found I wanted to be quieter, humbler, and kinder.

Being alone has never been a problem for me. I liked to be alone as a child, and it was even more important in the months after Mac died. It gave me time to think, plan, talk, and most importantly, listen to God. It became so important to spend the time alone in silence that I even questioned whether I really needed cable TV. I needed the silence to hear God.

It was also in the second year when I felt God had been preparing me beforehand for Mac's death. To this day I find that to be profound. I had been having thoughts of what it would be like without Mac. He was becoming more distant, and I was becoming more independent. I never wished he would die, so I didn't feel guilty by thinking I had contributed to his death by having those thoughts. But it was more as if God was preparing me for it, even though I didn't know it at the time.

And there were other hints: I had an urge to read C.S. Lewis and Anne Morrow Lindbergh. Both authors have written about their experiences with death. Our last vacation together, just weeks before he died, was spent on Sanibel Island in Florida, a favorite of Anne Morrow Lindbergh.

Lewis wrote: "When we lose one blessing, another is often most unexpectedly given in its place." I think he was right. And in Lewis' book, *The Problem of Pain*, he said: "God whispers to us in our pleasures, speaks in our conscience, but shouts in our pains: it is His megaphone to rouse a deaf world." The death helped me refocus and listen to God working in and through my life. I also became aware of Anne Wilson Schaef during my second year of grief (I had never read her before). In her writing about grief and pain, she said, "Only in feeling them do I open myself to the lessons they can teach." I could relate.

Sometimes it seemed like God's answers came months later. While looking for a full-time job after I was laid off, I decided to take on a part-time job. The training was such that you needed to "get it" within three days. Frankly, it was quite hard at the time for me to learn anything new within a few days.

And to make matters worse, I had been in a fender-bender the week before which I was trying to get resolved. Not learning everything quickly was devastating, even though the job was nothing to write home about.

It wasn't until months later, after I was back at the college as a learning specialist with an "expertise" in writing, that it dawned on me what value that earlier experience had. It made me a more compassionate educator. I told students I would explain things as many times as they needed, and I assured them they would "get it" eventually. I wanted everyone to reach that point some day. It takes time. I think God planned that temporary job to help me with the purpose he had for me—a full-time job that allowed me to use much more of my strengths and abilities.

God also lead me to Bible studying at Westminster by the Sea Presbyterian Church, where I am a member. The Bible has given me hope even in the middle of mourning and that hope can bring joy. In 1 Peter 1:6 (NIV), Peter reminds us we may "suffer grief in all kinds of trials." Those trials helped me see things differently. I now believe God has taken the brokenness of my life and has directed me to others who are broken. Like a sculpture, He is making me into a new person, chipping away some of my rougher edges.

CHAPTER 3.

Thanksgiving and Other Important Days We Shared

I will lift up mine eyes unto the hills... —Psalm 121 (KJV)

Our marriage in October 1991 was at an open-air chapel in the Blue Ridge Mountains in South Carolina. Above the chapel was engraved the line from Psalm 121—"I will lift up mine eyes unto the hills." My friend, Ann, and I went there for the first wedding anniversary after Mac's death. I wanted to return some of his ashes. It was a memorable experience, and I thought it was important to do so. I'm thinking, however, it's unlikely I will return there again, even though I keep getting drawn back there. One thing I'm starting to learn in the second year is to stop using the word "never."

The second wedding anniversary after Mac died was a normal working day for me. I was awaiting the birth of my nephew, Brian, and his wife Sylvia's first baby. I was pleased with the normalcy and the excitement of a new life. One special thing did happen, however. A colleague left a voice mail saying Mac's name was mentioned during a local Rotary meeting, and that Mac was still on the minds of others. That colleague had no way of knowing that day would have been our twenty-fourth anniversary. It turned out to be a very special voice mail. Little reminders from others of our loved one is always special.

Many widows find anniversaries tough days to get through, especially if they were memorable. Ours always were. We traditionally would take a vacation around our anniversary. I'm still considering what to do, if anything, in October. I've come to appreciate all the special days that Mac and I shared. It took almost two years of cycling through the "anniversaries" to see it as a way to process my pain and loss, a little more each year. I am now calmly moving on, remembering more of the good times that we shared.

By the second year and still grieving, I had an overwhelming desire to plan "something" on those special days including Valentine's Day, his birthday (April 30), my birthday (June 15), our anniversary (October 19), and Christmas. So I listened to God for direction.

Mac died on November 28th, but I have chosen to acknowledge his death on Thanksgiving because he died on Thanksgiving Day. The first Thanksgiving after Mac's death, I spent it with Mac's brother and his family. It was important for me to be with Mac's loved ones for that first anniversary of his death. But again, it did not seem like it should be a reoccurring visit. I liked the idea of going somewhere to reflect and be thankful for all my blessings. Or at least that's what I was thinking then.

Since Mac's death, Christmas as a Christian holiday has become even more important. I love our service at Westminster By the Sea Presbyterian Church. It was a very grateful time for me the second year. I don't remember much about the Christmas that followed his death, less than a month earlier. I was in shock. Nothing was the least bit merry. And I was still trying to figure out what needed to be done. I was truly lost. By the second year that turned into thankfulness.

Christmas Eve a year later brought one familiar sign: the "Yes, Virginia, there is a Santa Claus" letter to the editor in the *Daytona Beach News Journal*. Mac was the opinion editor at the paper at the time of his death. He always liked to run that letter, first published in the 1897 *The New York Sun*. It's nice to see the tradition continue. Mac and I loved to open gifts the first minute after midnight on Christmas morning. I plan to wish Mac a Merry Christmas at that time and read "Yes, Virginia, there is a Santa Claus" if I can stay up that late. He was truly a special gift in my life.

The Throwers sent a Kindle gift card the second Christmas, recalling the Kindle that Mac gave me several years earlier, and how he left his credit card number on the account for all the books I wanted ordered. "I think he may be smiling right now," his brother said. I thanked him for the gift card and jokingly asked him for his credit card number. The Throwers are good folk.

A new tradition I have started is adding white garlands with Christmas ornaments we collected on our travels. The first garland I worked on went above the fireplace mantle. Another new tradition I have started, however, is buying new PJs each Christmas season. Sitting around the house in PJs is fun and relaxing, not to mention good clothes to write in. I did that on the second New Year's after his death, putting away Christmas decorations, watching parades and football games. But mostly, I was relaxing. I was especially touched with the Donate Life Rose Parade float.

Mac's eyes had been donated, so it reminded me of the first Valentine's Day after his death when I received a beautiful medal from the donor group that had accepted Mac's eyes. It was a wonderful surprise especially on that day. Also, on Valentine's Day, I decided I would like to start reading the many cards Mac gave me that I have saved over the years. He never missed giving cards on the important days, and I saved all of them. That has helped me through the grief.

What I don't plan to continue is the Southern tradition of black-eyed peas and greens for New Year's. Mac was faithful to that tradition, but it will be one I will take a pass on. I'm not one who relies on tradition to bring me good luck.

Mac's birthday was in April. We always had a nice meal to celebrate. For his first and second birthday after his death, Ann and I went out to dinner. The first year we took some ashes to spread at one of the favorite Atlantic

Coast islands Mac and I loved to visit. The second year I was in Daytona Beach and working, so we went out for dinner and drinks after work. I saw this activity as just another sign I was starting to integrate Mac's memories into my new lifestyle.

Now, I'm thinking of doing something different to celebrate his birthday. Mac was an English major, and I learned a lot about literature from him. In the second year, I started reading a play from Shakespeare in honor of Mac. It would make him smile.

My birthday in June is becoming a "wing it" weekend with my best friend. The first year, we went to Miami Beach for my sixtieth birthday, which was fun. The second year, we returned to the North Carolina mountains for a long weekend.

The first Fourth of July after Mac died, my best friend wanted to celebrate my sixtieth birthday in New York City. It was a wonderful and memorable time. By the second Fourth of July, I was home in my apartment, turning down a long-weekend trip to the mountains. I was craving some time alone.

Mac loved fireworks, and although I didn't dwell on the Fourth of July celebrations from years past, I did smile as I recalled a couple of events we enjoyed in Mobile, Alabama, and St. Louis, Missouri. In Mobile, the fireworks appeared like magic as we emerged from a tunnel along Interstate 10. And in St. Louis from our suburban hotel room several stories up, we could see fireworks all around the greater St. Louis area. It was awesome! The memories and smiles were starting to kick in.

CHAPTER 4.

Help From Friends and What to Say to Them

"Pride leads to every other vice: it is the complete anti-God state of mind." —C. S. Lewis

Mac and I were childless, in part, because we were in our late 30s when we married and because Mac had a serious heart condition. So, the connection I have with friends became even stronger after he died. I have relied a lot on them while also trying to maintain a healthy independence. All widows deal with the question others are thinking, which is "Should they bring up your late spouse's name in your presence?" The answer for me is a resounding "yes" but just as an interjection or short story. I liked to hear Mac stories, but I didn't want our whole conversation to be only about Mac and my grief.

I found it was easier to bring up Mac's name myself because people are reluctant to do so. Friends seemed concerned about upsetting me. But for me, it was a way for a friend to acknowledge Mac and a way for me to talk about him; it was a win-win moment. I wanted to share my grief, but I didn't want to share too much of myself with people who I didn't know well. That was a bit of a balancing act for me and one I didn't want my pride to get in the way of. I didn't want people to feel sorry for me, yet I wanted to talk about what I was going through.

Most widows, in the days after their husbands have died, don't want to hear "he's free from suffering" or similar remarks. It's too soon for that. I thought Raymond R. Mitsch and Lynn Brookside in *Grieving the Loss of Someone You Love: Daily Meditations to Help You Through the Grieving Process* had a good response to such comments: "That doesn't make it any easier for me right now. I still hurt terribly. But you're right. That will be a great comfort to me in the future, once this terrible sorrow has run the course." They suggest you then thank them and move on. "You'll feel better and heal better for having provided some balance for the truth," they say.

I'm finding that the longer I'm a widow, the more comfortable people are talking about Mac. It's almost as if people seem to think you are okay about talking about your spouse after a year or two. Some of my long-time friends wanted to talk about Mac from the day he died.

I have kept many of my "old" friends whom, in some cases, Mac and I knew. But I have also added new friends, some I would never have thought would be friends, because before Mac died, I wasn't open to making new friends outside my small circle. Now, I like having friends from different places. Some of my friends know each other and some don't.

Ann, who I had only known a couple of years, was the first friend I called the day Mac died. She was there whenever I needed her. And our closeness grew. But some people didn't even realize their impact. Take, for example, Barbara, a "cleaning lady" at Daytona State College. She had lost her husband about the same time that Mac died. She taught me that we all meet in a place called grief regardless of our backgrounds.

And then there was Cathy from church. Early on after Mac died, she asked if she could sit with me in church. About a year after Mac died, she reminded me not to feel guilty as I started to feel happier. A group of younger co-workers at the college have been especially helpful. Several of them had recently lost parents. Except Ann, the friends at work are either single or divorced. So their losses of a parent or spouse were different from mine. But it was still a loss.

I also plan to stay in touch with Mac's friends and family. Mac and I always spent part of the holidays with his only brother, George. So, I hope to stay connected but probably not as much as my life goes in a new direction. In April of the second year, they wanted to come down from Charlotte for a long weekend. We planned the weekend close to what would have been Mac's sixty-second birthday. I had visited them in November on the first anniversary of his death and now it was time for them to see my new living arrangements. I have to say, the visit was bittersweet for me. Mac's sixty-second birthday was not nearly as trying for me as the sixty-first birthday, the first one after he died. By the time the second birthday after his death came along, I couldn't help but think that I had started to move on, surely a lot more than I had a year earlier. It felt to me like George was still doing his own mourning, and I was a reminder. The entire weekend of that second birthday seemed very sad. By then, almost a year and a half after his death, I was feeling more and more comfortable telling stories about Mac and really feeling like they were blending into happy memories. But I didn't think George and I were on the same page.

Time will tell how much we will spend together. At the moment, I'm thinking maybe a lunch, or at the most, an overnight visit might be the way to go.

Mac's death has brought a heightened awareness of the suffering of others. Because of my experience and help from friends, I'm beginning to learn how to better respond to people dealing with the long-term illness of loved ones. An acquaintance from church taught me what to say to someone who says "I don't know how I am going to go on without you." The response was: "You're going to spread the love you've had for me around so others can also enjoy it."

This wise acquaintance was an eighty-something member of my grief group at church. That group, and a Bible study group I also shared with him, really brought home the reality that as we experience the separation of a loved one, we become connected to those who have a similar loss. I remember one Sunday we both had tears in our eyes for different reasons. A Bible passage reminded him of his wife. My tears came from thinking about a minister I hadn't seen in months who was dying from cancer. One of the last funerals he presided over was for Mac. While the Bible study group had some people closer to my age, the grief group had people much older, but I still felt a closeness, even if we were coming at the grief from different ages. We had all been through a life-changing experience that we all could relate to.

And then there was Ponce, the dark gray cat Mac bought me as a Christmas present two years before he died. Ponce was a replacement for our beloved Cookie, who was with us eighteen years. Yes, Ponce and I would talk. Well, I would talk to Ponce. He really has never been one to *meow* much, and I felt we did get closer after Mac died.

CHAPTER 5.

Mac Moments

M emories seem to pop up at odd times. I call them "Mac Moments." There were times when it seemed like almost everything had some kind of meaning. In the spring of 2015, I watched a TV documentary on Japanese cherry blossoms. A cherry blossom tree just happened to be one of the first trees that Mac planted at our first home. The segment said that in Japan, the blossoms signify that time on earth is brief and that it should be lived gloriously. I thought that said so much about Mac's life. And it made me think about planting a cherry tree in his honor somewhere, although I still haven't decided where. The cherry blossom is just one of many examples of how Mac Moments come out of nowhere.

At one point around the holidays, I was sitting at home when I started to think about Mac's glasses. I had donated them through our church not long after his death, but for some reason I wanted to think about those glasses. Mac requested that his organs be donated, and it was his beautiful blue eyes that were taken. Now whenever I think of sight, I think of those eyes and glasses.

In another pop-up memory, I was watching the movie, *Ghandi*, and the reporter in the movie had a hat like Mac used to wear. Still in another pop-up memory, I was driving down the street when I saw a Honda that was the same blue color of the first Honda Mac bought after we were married. Many come quickly and leave quickly. At first, those moments brought sadness as I thought about my loss. But I'm beginning to see the transition from sorrow to memories.

When Mac was still alive, the paper where he worked at started a massive tree-clearing project in front of the newspaper office. In February, more than a year after his death, the project was completed. I couldn't help but think what Mac would have thought about it—all those beautiful trees that hid the newspaper's building had been replaced with open lots that could potentially be subdivided into a strip mall or car lot along busy Nova Road. There is no doubt Mac would have preferred the trees.

And then there were stories in the paper that led me to think of Mac. During the second year after his death, his cousins in nearby DeLand sold some commercial property for a new hotel which I found out about in the newspaper. It reminded me of how wonderful Mac's cousins were before and at the time of his death.

Because Mac had such a public job as a journalist, I've accepted there will be times when his work will be mentioned or shown in writing. That's what happened near the two-year anniversary of his death. While I'm not a big Facebook user, I do like to see what others are saying. On one particular day in early November 2015, a group of people with connections to *The Greenville News*—the paper where we had met—were circulating a page from the paper with all the awards given twenty-five years earlier. Mac's award for editorial writing was among them. It also happened to be the year we were engaged, and it was such an exciting time for us.

Even Ponce's vet visit brought back a Mac Moment. Mac came with me to that same vet one summer day in 2011 to put our first cat, Cookie, to sleep after we had exhausted all hope for her recovery. We had her cremated, and when I showed Mac a piece of her fur, it brought tears, a rarity for Mac.

In Jerry L. Sittser's book, *A Grace Disguised: How the Soul Grows Through Loss*, he talks about "phantom pains" or reminders of a former life that may appear in surprising ways. One was quite funny for me. It involved the birds at the Port Orange Library. It seemed some mother birds were pecking people as they entered the entrance at the library because they thought the patrons were getting too close to their nests. I couldn't help but think that Mac, who always loved birds, arranged for the pecking birds at the same time I was dropping off some of his books. He found books impossible to part with. When I was completing my taxes in 2015, I found I had donated almost 500 books. There were other reminders involving birds. Anytime I now see a Roseate Spoonbill or eagle, I think of him. He loved birdfeeders and watching birds that would come to them. He fed birds up until the day he died. And every time I see a birdfeeder in the store, thoughts of Mac come up and bring a smile.

Sometimes the phantom memories would come at odd times. I remember one time staying at a hotel where a set of drawers looked just like the set Mac had from his childhood, a set that stayed with him until his death. During the singing of "America the Beautiful" during the 2015 Super Bowl in Arizona, the stadium screen showed pictures of the Grand Canyon and Seattle. Those were two areas (Seattle as the starting point for an Alaskan cruise) Mac said he wanted to visit after his artificial valve operation. I have always been comforted knowing that Mac was able to visit both with me.

But we were not able to do everything. Mac always wanted to own a kayak, but that never happened. I had finally agreed to go on a kayak trip the year he died, and I arranged for the trip. But, unfortunately, we were never able to go.

Our favorite song while dating was "I Don't Know Much," written by Barry Mann and Cynthia Weil. Several months after Mac died, when Ann and I decided to go to New York City for a long weekend, we wanted to take in some live theater. We chose *Beautiful*, the story of Carole King. I didn't realize until months later that Mann and Weil were an important part of the play because of their friendship and competition with King.

And then there are the "Mac Moment" emails from events that we experienced together. I remember around the holidays I saw an email from the

Experimental Aircraft Association (EAA) that brought the Ford Tri-Motor airplane to New Smyrna Beach. The plane was known as the first mass-produced airliner from aviation's formative years. One of the best gifts I ever gave Mac was an EAA ride, which he loved.

I went by New Smyrna Beach Municipal Airport (Jack Bolt Field) in February and had to smile because there sat the Goodyear blimp. It was in town for the Daytona 500. The blimp would fly over our house near Daytona Beach during race week. We loved to go outside and watch as it made its way to hover over the track. A hot air balloon event at that same airport was advertising the appearance of a B-17 World War II fighter bomber. There is no doubt Mac would have wanted to go see it. He loved old planes.

I imagine all widows experience their loved ones' names on outdated mailing lists. I had to remind my auto insurer that Mac was no longer a second driver, even though I wasn't paying for a second driver.

Mac loved golf—both to play and to watch. And he especially loved golf during March when the professionals came to Florida. He was able to see the pros in Jacksonville and Orlando. So, when the events are advertised in March, it brings on Mac Moments. One event I will always remember is when Mac shouted out to Ernie Ells that he had made a good shot. Ells looked at him and tipped his hat. Mac looked like an elated child.

He would have loved the 2015 British Open in St. Andrews, Scotland. We had made the trip to Scotland and St. Andrews in 1997. At the 2015 Open in July, Tom Watson made his final appearance. And there at the end was Ernie Ells. This was another Mac Moment. He also would have loved The Players tournament in Jacksonville in 2015 that went into "Sudden Death." I could see him there watching the playoffs with me. And I could just about guess who he would have been rooting for.

I learned to love golf from Mac. And although it's not my favorite sport, it is a sport we enjoyed together. I see myself phasing golf out of my life. I still have my clubs, but probably won't keep them forever. The same is true for watching the big golf events. I still like to see them but that probably won't last either. That is something we shared, and it will never be the same without him.

Mac was a huge Duke University basketball fan, so when they went to the Final Four in 2015, I decided to text his brother and wife during the game. It was the next best thing to having him there. Mac would have loved the final game between Duke and Wisconsin. I found it ironic—and to some degree apropos—that Duke was playing in Indianapolis, a city we loved visiting. But it was also in 1991—the year we got married—that Duke won the national title there. I felt Mac was there watching Duke win again, twenty-four years later. I could see him so excited and yelling "yes" at every good basket. He would have watched every minute. He was in my thoughts as I watched the game from my apartment.

We loved to share good food and good restaurants. And when I find good food I know he would have loved—like good summer rolls—I can't help but think how much he would have loved them. When we lived in Paducah, Kentucky, we would travel more than 100 miles to Nashville, in part, to get summer rolls at a restaurant we loved. It was more than a year after his death when I found out a grocery store, about a mile from where we lived, had wonderful summer rolls as good as the ones we found in Nashville. He didn't live long enough to discover them.

And watching the Kentucky Derby brought tears the second year after he died, especially when "My Old Kentucky Home" was played. We had an 1860s Antebellum home in Kentucky. And that song always reminds me of our eight-year stay there.

As time goes on, I'm finding the Mac Moments farther apart, but I know they will never disappear. They will always remain as a way of remembering Mac.

CHAPTER 6.

The Stuff

W hat do you do with all the stuff you no longer need? Some things were obvious. Mac's nice suits went to the Men and Women's Center at the college where I work to be given to students who need to look nice for job interviews. I took his glasses to the charity that collects them through my church. His camera went to the Photography Department at the college, and lots of clothes I took to Goodwill.

There is no way to know where his clothes ended up. But one cold winter day while working at the college, I saw a man who had on a jacket that looked like one of Mac's. I knew from talking to him that he had come on hard times and was now returning to college. I also knew he had been a writer while in the service. I would have liked to believe that's where that jacket ended up.

Clothes that were gifts to me from Mac have been very hard to give up. Many of them were quite expensive and nice. I had a green and red plaid, flannel shirt that was adorable. Over the years, it was no longer useful, but it was hard to give away.

But what about those other special things, especially those things that had a special connection between us? I have several pieces of jewelry I want to recreate. I've started with a diamond from an earring set he gave me. I asked a local jeweler to put that on a gold flip-flop my best friend gave me. It reminds me of two special people.

I still haven't decided what to do with the diamond engagement ring. I might recreate it into some other piece, but I'm just not sure yet. I read one suggestion that says "If it makes you smile, keep it," so I've been using that approach as I continue to downsize.

What to do with some things comes immediately, while other things I struggle with. The handcrafted dulcimer Mac gave me for our first anniversary is one of those things. We had a dulcimer player at our wedding, so that made the "what to do" question even greater. Obviously, it's a keeper, but where? It's funny. The dulcimer could very well be a permanent part of my life. It remains a conversation piece on top of an antique armoire we both loved.

There are some items I will just keep until the right idea pops into my head, such was the case with Mac's awards. Mac had received many awards, and most of them had the traditional wooden backs. One day, I emailed the police chief in Daytona Beach and asked if I could donate them to the Special Olympics, a group the police department was involved with. The idea was to use the wooden backs for their awards. He was thrilled, and they are now being used with a group that was close to Mac's heart. Trust the silence.

Mac came home with a homemade rug one day from a craft show at work. It was always an important part of where we lived. I especially liked the fact that Mac had picked it, but it had become worn and faded over twenty-something years. I didn't really want to display it anymore, even though I did for more than a year after he died. It took another year to come up with a new idea for the rug. It will now be used in my hatchback car to cover up items I don't want people to see from the outside.

Transitioning

Mac was a big person in many respects. He liked things big, especially electronics. So, the fifty-five-inch TV was a comfortable reminder until it suddenly stopped. I elected not to get it fixed and opted for a smaller size. Since everything was getting smaller, including my living space, I was left with a rather large TV console, which I advertised on Craigslist. On a very early Sunday morning, four days before Christmas, a woman from Haiti and her moving friend arrived from Orlando to purchase my heavy seventy-seven-inch console. Any fear of dealing with strangers immediately left as the very small couple maneuvered the heavy piece onto an old pickup and headed home but not before helping me rearrange my remaining furniture. I must admit, I have had good luck with Craigslist. And in some cases, it created some interesting stories, like when I sold Mac's guitar. It turned out to be the husband of an editor at the paper where he worked who answered the ad.

Another Craigslist item that I listed was a treadmill. I loved the treadmill, but I was becoming more of a walker outside and with a friend, instead of inside my place by myself. After all, I do live in Florida. When Mac was still alive, our routine was for me to get up early and use the treadmill before he woke up. On the morning Mac died, I decided not to do the treadmill. Instead, I sat in the living room reading the paper. I was doing this when Mac screamed out from the heart attack he was having while still in bed.

Of course, I heard the scream and immediately went in to help and called 911. I have often thought what would have happened if I had done my treadmill routine. It would have been at least an hour before I realized anything was wrong, or maybe even longer, since it was a holiday (Thanksgiving), and Mac didn't have to get up for work. On one hand, I wouldn't have heard the scream and may have always thought he died in his sleep. But I do have the comfort of knowing I did everything I could, even though he never responded to my efforts. I would like to think at least he could hear everything I was doing to get help.

A few weeks before Mac died, he received a calendar from his alma mater, Belmont Abbey College in Belmont, North Carolina. It stretched from November 2013 until December 2014. The November month had no entries. But after his death on November 28, I used the calendar for the next fourteen months to plan everything I had to do, including three garage sales, selling numerous items on Craigslist, and organizing all the clips Mac had written during his more than thirty-year career in the newspaper business, mostly as an editorial writer.

In January, after the first anniversary of his death passed, I decided to throw away the calendar, except for the November 2013 month. I'm not sure at this point what I will do with that page. But something will come up some day. Things I decided to save a year ago now seem to be ready for the giveaway, sell, or throwaway pile. Such was the case with the cat toys. Unless they broke, we never threw away any of Cookie's toys. I had a box of toys with some that had not been used very much. I spent the better part of several weeks seeing if Ponce wanted any of the existing toys. He did pick a few. But most were thrown out with the trash. The same person I had three joint yard sales with the first year had another yard sale the second year. I had very little to offer, and most of it turned out to be better for donating than selling.

Much of the furniture has been replaced, with the exception of a few key pieces I plan to keep. While some people find comfort in having "his" chair and other items around them, I found I had a mixture of wanting some items to stay and some to move on. A local Catholic charity picked up the bed Mac had the heart attack in. That happened about five months after he died. I had been sleeping in the guestroom except when visitors would come, and they would stay in the guest room. I never felt comfortable in our bed again. For me, giving the bed away was a way of acknowledging that he was gone. But that was not the case initially for a sofa and recliner we had bought for a first house more than twenty years ago. The two pieces were comforting in the months after Mac died. But the time seemed right during spring break more than a year later to replace them. I had the same Catholic charity pick those up. Trust your inner voice.

As I've downsized, I've tried to continue getting rid of items as I collect new ones. That's rather hard to do since Mac and I always had plenty of room for clutter. It's amazing how easy it is to find things now. And it's even more amazing that I have not missed anything I sold or gave away so far. I am nearing the two-year mark, and I'm finding so little that I really need.

The next phase will be to start sorting out the photos, newspaper clips, and other memories into some organized method, but I look at that as a long-term project that I can work on at a snail's pace.

CHAPTER 7.

Changing Habits

"I keep on through habit fitting an arrow to the string; then
I remember and have to lay the bow down." —C.S. Lewis,
A Grief Observed

I was still sleeping on the left side of the bed well into the second year after
Mac died. That's just one of the many habits that I'm still doing, and it's
taking some time to break this habit. But I'm confident I'll know when to
change or maybe not change. With some other things, I really didn't have
a choice. It seems so odd putting "widow" now on anything that requires a
classification. I don't see myself as a widow, even though there is no doubt
that I am. I know I must adjust. I believe it takes well into the second year of
being a widow to feel the impact of everything that must change. All aspects
of my life are involved. Everything now is about me and not about us, and
that took time to grasp.

Somewhere during that second year, I adopted a new attitude toward
change. And it seemed to be the natural next step. First, I accepted that
change was part of the process of recovering from grief. Secondly, I accepted
that a change in behavior begins with my heart changing, and in my case,

with help from God. Thirdly, I believed a new and fresh opportunity with life would come with this change.

During the first year, change seemed like it was constant, since I had so much to do, including selling a house, selling two old cars and buying a newer one. Did I mention downsizing? Now three garage sales later, I'm settled in a comfortable, albeit small, apartment that fits my needs. Much of my artwork in the apartment reminds me of Mac and places we have been. It all brings back great memories, and I like having it around. But I'm not obsessed with it; I'm comforted by it.

One Sunday morning in January during the second year, I decided to hang a picture given to me by a dear friend. It was a picture that Mac didn't particularly like, but I loved it. Putting the picture up was symbolic of the ongoing changes as I transitioned into my new life. On my walls are a few blank spaces ready for new pictures or objects that will be a part of my new life. I've already added one new picture, a lithograph, of Sloppy Joe's in Key West. While I bought it on an antiquing trip with Ann and her husband, it also reminded me of Mac, since we had been to the Keys together where we visited Sloppy Joe's.

I've always liked the idea of aromatherapy. Since Mac died, I've been even more into candles and other smells. Yes, it's calming, but it's also another sign of something uniquely me.

Downsizing was something I wanted to do for simplicity reasons. Although I could afford a larger place, I wanted something smaller. At first I worried what people would think about me. Did Mac leave me very little? Did I have to declare bankruptcy? Neither was the case, but it didn't stop the worrying. Then I thought back on my life, and I remembered that I had always been unique. And it was that "uniqueness" that was a blessing from God. It didn't matter what others thought.

Other changes were more related directly to Mac. I remember visiting an outlet mall near St. Augustine, Florida, the first time after Mac's death. We liked to visit that mall, especially the Brooks Brothers store. I could still go to Gander Mountain and other stores, but I no longer had anything to buy at Brooks Brothers, so I made the decision to stop going there.

Another habit both of us loved was reading the daily newspaper. We had met when I was a reporter and Mac was an editor at a paper in South Carolina. I had loved reading a daily newspaper years before I met Mac. After Mac died, I continued to read the local daily paper where Mac had been the opinion editor, but as time passed, I realized, like so many other people, that I no longer needed to read a daily newspaper. I was also looking to change my morning habits. I had started integrating Bible reading and reflection in the morning, so I unsubscribed to the newspaper for a while. Then I changed my mind. Now I'm reading the paper again. That one goes back and forth. What keeps me going back to the paper is the need for local news. It's also a nice memory of my former profession.

I've been reading a lot about how important it is to experience the grief rather than always keeping busy and not confronting the grief. This is a tough one for me because I am one of those people who likes projects. I have worked all my adult life, mostly in professional education and writing jobs. Returning to work, especially after the first Christmas without Mac, helped me stay anchored. But I could sense things were changing. I was more interested in what matters in my personal life. And then I was told four months after Mac died that my job was ending in three months. The two "events" back to back were devastating, even though Mac's death by far was the worst of the two. Oddly, because I now had to look for a new job at age 60, it gave me a new purpose with less time to think about only being a widow. At times, it almost seemed like a blessing that I now had time to grieve without being at work, even though my day included a lot of time looking for jobs. I stayed unemployed for ten weeks, and they were some of the most life-building, thought-provoking ten weeks of my life. I started looking at my life and all the things I still wanted to achieve. I started to do volunteer work and found it a broadening experience.

I also picked up some odds and ends jobs, like working the Daytona 500 race in February, more for the excitement than the money. And that it was. I met people from all over the world as a greeter. By the time I worked the NASCAR race, I had returned to the college full-time, this time as a learning specialist in the Academic Support Center. After working the 500, I found I really appreciated my "day job" because I learned a lot of people work very hard for a living and not necessarily doing what they would like to do. I'm not sure I have the endurance to stand on my feet twelve hours per day all week long, but I found I could do it for two days in a row during the races. I've been lucky and blessed in that I've always had jobs I've enjoyed.

Starting new routines is something I have struggled with, but the second year seemed to start bringing things into focus. Because Mac died in bed as he was waking up, the first few minutes of the morning I now set aside as a time of gratitude. I always thank God I'm alive and then spend a few minutes reading from the Bible. My day then begins. Part of the second-year grieving process for me is to establish a place to go and reflect on a regular basis. That's easy for me since I live in a beach area near Daytona Beach, Florida. I can be on the beach in ten minutes from my place. And my church is two blocks from the beach. I've added ongoing Bible study to my new routine, and I would like to someday go to the Holy Land to cap off my understanding of the Bible. In the Spring, I added reading Shakespeare to my reading list. And in the Fall, I began reading the classics, starting with Moby Dick. My goal is to always have a classic that I'm reading. Reading the classics makes me appreciate good writing.

CHAPTER 8.

Moving On After Taking Time to Grieve

For, lo, the winter is past,
The rain is over and gone;
The flowers appear on the earth;
The time of the singing of birds is come,
And the voice of the turtle is heard in the land.
—Song of Solomon 2:11-12 (KJV)

I am now convinced that people do not entirely "get over grief." It becomes part of life's normal, healthy healing process. And, ultimately, a widow begins to integrate that grief into one's new life. Wisdom does come from the experience. If you're fortunate, God helps one apply that wisdom. Getting to that point, however, doesn't come easy. One of the decisions I thought I had to make was to stop grieving, but I learned that it was not something I could just stop. I started to change gradually, feeling more at peace, more comfortable and more able to wait for the next step to happen.

It all started coming together well into the second year after Mac died. Except for a few setbacks now and then, I started to see more clearly what it would be like to have a life without Mac by my side. That is, a life that would integrate all our experiences into a new life for me. What really stood out was that I now had a better perspective on life's ups and downs.

It started to make sense when I read The *Way of Serenity* by Father Jonathan Morris. In the book, Father Morris talks about "discernment of spirits," a term he borrowed from Ignatius of Loyola, the founder of the Jesuits. Basically, it's the action of God in our souls leading us in a certain direction. I had faced death, and now I had a new and deeper way of looking at my own life. I found the experience had enhanced my spiritual life. The experience made me appreciate living and helped me to be more patient and accepting of others. Oddly, it's like a part of me had died and a new part was evolving— one that was quieter and more contemplative. I was also less competitive, yet I started thinking of things I wanted to do that were far beyond the boundaries I had thought I could achieve.

I began to listen for signs of what direction to take and then let life take over. I don't think I'm out there like someone drifting with nowhere to go. I'm doing things, and in some cases, doing more than before and making plans for the long-term. I've resisted being a "victim" my entire life. I wasn't comfortable seeing myself as a victim. I didn't want people to feel sorry for me, and maybe that helps me on this journey.

In *From One Widow to Another: Conversations on the New You*, author Miriam Neff says that if you pushed your boundaries with little fear as an adolescent and carried that into your adult years, fear as a widow would likely not be debilitating. I thought she was speaking to me because I always liked the challenge of a new situation. Just ask my parents about my decision to head to Australia, with all I had to my name was $600 in travelers' checks and a just-completed education degree. I was twenty-one. Although I had plenty to worry about as a widow, I have never been one to dwell on fear. "We can choose the direction and whether it is positive or negative," Neff states.

One can't help feeling a little odd, however, about starting to enjoy life and not prolonging the grieving process. "What we want is to live our marriage well and faithfully through that phase too," said C.S. Lewis. For me it seemed almost irreverent to start enjoying life again. I would read stories of devoted spouses delivering flowers to loved ones' gravesites every day. I wanted Mac to be remembered, but I couldn't see myself doing that. Instead, I'm gradually adding items in honor of Mac as the need arises. For example, a new library at my church needed a new twelve-volume set of *The New Interpreter's Bible*, a perfect memorial with some of the money left from the "in lieu of flowers" request when Mac died.

With three-fourths of Mac's ashes scattered, I'm left wondering what I should do with those that remain. I've thought of keeping some close by so I can have a part of him go with me when I die. I'm also leaning toward planting a tree in his honor and placing them there. A part of me could join him there when I die, and meanwhile I will have a local place (and tree) to visit. (Note: I ended up putting the remaining ashes at my church's scatter garden where my ashes will also be placed.)

With time, I understand that the best memorial I can make for Mac is to move on with my own life by becoming a better person and integrating his memory into this new life. It's almost like he is watching from afar. I finally got it. Although Mac's loss and our time together will always be a part of my life, I wasn't going to let "our" life totally control my future. That attitude has allowed me to start to identify a new life for myself.

I've begun to prepare for the future. I come from a farming family from central Michigan, and I know all too well the importance of preparing the soil for the crop. My father was an expert at that. The same can be said for the next stage of one's life after the death of a spouse. I knew I first had to get rid of any excess baggage I still had from our marriage. I was not one to talk about problems a lot, especially as Mac's heart condition became worse, but I wished we had talked more about his health issues. We struggled financially through the newspaper crisis/recession starting in 2007. Neither of us ever lost our newspaper jobs, even though we were asked to take monetary cuts, like everyone else, in order to keep our jobs. But I know Mac worried about it constantly, especially about getting laid off. I'm glad he never did. But I will always believe the stress of the times contributed to his early death.

I vowed not to stay in newspapers when we moved to Florida. I'm glad in many ways I decided to return to the academic world. While it would have been unlikely that Mac and I would have been able to work together at the newspaper in Daytona Beach because of nepotism rules, I am grateful that I had my own world—with my own friends—at the time of his death. That was better for me. And while I did have some regrets for not doing more in our marriage—I understand all people do—I have elected to move on and not let those regrets weigh me down at this point.

I read somewhere that often, people who experience loss find a way to redefine themselves, and I found that was the case with me. It dawned on me recently that it had been years since I had quit a job because I was pursuing something new for myself. Three of the last four jobs were because Mac had found a new job, and I was limited geographically to where I could work. The last time I quit a job to take a better job just for myself was almost thirty years earlier. Wow!! The whole experience of Mac's death and the aftermath is allowing me to look at possible new careers and new ways to be creative. I'm finding I'm exploring alternatives again, and this time I'm thinking beyond my boundaries.

CHAPTER 9.

Importance of God

I saiah's words speak of a changed heart and a renewed spirit that come by receiving God's crown of beauty instead of ashes, the oil of joy instead of mourning, and a garment of praise instead of a spirit of despair. They will be called oaks of righteousness, a planting of the LORD for the display of his splendor (Isaiah 61:3, NIV).

I have never considered myself a religious person. Yes, I was brought up Catholic and went to a Catholic school for eight years back when nuns taught most of the classes, but for many years as an adult, I didn't attend church. During most of my marriage to Mac, we never attended church together, although we talked about it many times.

It wasn't until 2011, after we moved to the Daytona Beach area, that I finally insisted we were going to find a church. Mac attended a Catholic elementary school and graduated from a Catholic college, but he always considered himself Presbyterian, in part, because of his Scottish heritage. I was always oaky with becoming a Presbyterian. So we started exploring the various types of churches in the greater Daytona Beach area. We decided on Westminster by the Sea Presbyterian Church because of its traditional approach to worship. The decision to return to church I now think was driven by God who knew I would need His comfort, so I wouldn't walk through the grief alone.

Mac died waking up in the morning. I was nearby in the living room when I heard his loud scream. And he was gone that quickly. The scene has played out in my mind many times. For months, I thought of how much he must have suffered those last few seconds. God has helped me think past this difficult image. I now envision Mac being released from his pain and entering a new life. It took me more than a year, however, to think this way. This new vision came together for me on Good Friday, the day Christ died.

I knew having peace with God would not take away all my problems, but it did calm me. As Jesus said, "These things I have spoken unto you, that in me ye might have peace. In the world ye shall have tribulation: but be of good cheer; I have overcome the world." (John 16:33, KJV)

Another tribulation that second year was a health scare. My good health was somewhat tested on, of all days, my sixty-first birthday. I got news from my doctor that I needed to get a CT scan because of a spot on my lungs. I proceeded with the same hope that God would take over just as he had with the loss of Mac and the loss of my job. And he did. Everything turned out fine.

Almost immediately after Mac died, I felt I had more strongly found God. And the experience gave me a better sense of the truth I wanted to live by. But for me, the lost-and-found experience was a solitary experience. I started to realize that the grief I was experiencing was a chance to connect more to my spiritual potential, a side I ignored most of my married life.

My minister told me about a man who would not return to our church after the loss of his wife. He said he couldn't bear to come back after her funeral at the church. I have had the opposite experience in that I found I needed to go to church even more. I found comfort in the book of Romans when the apostle Paul said, "We can rejoice…when we run into problems and trials, for we know that they help us develop endurance. And endurance develops strength of character, and character strengthens our confident hope of salvation." (Romans 5:3, NLT)

I joined a weekly Bible study group about three months before the first-year anniversary of Mac's death. I have never really understood what compelled me to join; it wouldn't have even been on my radar a year earlier. I found that it had a calming effect on me. Shortly after the holidays, we were reading Job. It really spoke to me about trusting God and why bad things sometimes happen.

I find it especially calming to read the Bible while listening to classical music. I have always had classical music at home, but I had not been listening much to it in recent years. Studying the Bible with classical music has become a new interest of mine. The Bible words offer a spiritual renewal for me, like a refreshing look on life that offers food for thought. As in Isaiah 55:10: "As the rain and the snow come down from heaven, and do not return to it without watering the earth and making it bud and flourish so that it yields seed for the sower and bread for the eater…" (NIV)

To concentrate on studying the Bible every week is so different from hearing excerpts during Sunday services. It was a lot of reading—almost the whole Bible in a year—but it really started tying things together in my life. While a Bible study group was new, reading the Bible wasn't. In fact, I had been reading parts of the Bible daily prior to Mac's death, including the morning he died.

I see in my future helping those who have lost loved ones. But I'm also listening for other ideas God wants me to consider. So, like Saul on the way to Damascus, I'm asking God what I should do.

One possibility is to return to India. I spent six months there in my twenties as part of a year-long solo travel venture on my return home from teaching in Australia. It was such a fascinating country. The idea of returning with a purpose seems like a real possibility now.

CHAPTER 10.

Time

T ime used to go so fast. Now there is nothing but time. I've accepted that Mac's passing will always be a part of my being, and with time, it will be something that I can continue to gain knowledge from, and this knowledge may help others. I also hope it will continue to build my character. Ralph Waldo Emerson said, "Death puts life into perspective." I've learned, though, that I need to pace myself, especially when it comes to grief. I can't rush through the process even though there are times I wish I could.

Everything has changed, or at least it seems that way. Some things seem to not matter as much anymore, including having material items and wanting to succeed to higher positions. One big thing I've noticed is that I don't get as rattled anymore over what to me now seems like such trivial stuff that wasn't trivial when Mac was alive. For example, I now adjust to last-minute travel changes or traffic jams with little fanfare.

That approach to life comes in handy as an educator who daily must deal with the ups and downs of students. The job seems so much more enjoyable and satisfying. I once read that what defines us is not our job but how we rise under difficult circumstances, and sometimes circumstances are created for us. That is what happened to me the first year. Seven months after Mac died, my job was eliminated. While I wouldn't wish the "double whammy" on my worst enemy, it proved to be a valuable combination for me. The time that I initially thought would be very unsettling became a time of calming. And it really was a turning point as things began to become clearer in my life.

I didn't realize until months later that the ten weeks when I was laid off were a very valuable, contemplative time for me that allowed me to move forward. It gave me time to stop and grieve, something that proved to be invaluable. It also gave me time to think about the inevitable changes that had to come and what I wanted to see as the outcome. In looking back, I would not have had the time to do all that while working full-time.

I was eventually rehired by the same college in an even better position for me and my future. I came back to the college better healed and ready for the next chapter of my life. I saw the beginning of my journey without Mac like riding on a boat in a turbulent sea. At first, it seemed like all I could do was stay afloat. At times, I had no energy to steer the boat. But as time passed, the days became less turbulent, and I found myself steering more and more in the right direction. I felt a noticeable change about one and a half years after Mac died. I had settled into a simple, comfortable life. Most of the big decisions that were directly related to Mac's death had been made, and I started to think more and more about what I needed.

As the intensity of the grief passed, I soon realized the truth about Mac's death even clearer as I had read in *Healing After Loss*. "In the early stages we are preoccupied not with the memory of our loved one, but with our own pain," the book by Martha Whitmore Hickman said. As time went on, I thought of myself as less of a widow and more of an independent woman. I started to see more and more the things I could do. It has been very helpful for me to be mindful of or to concentrate on the present. That includes not worrying about matters that are beyond my control. When I start now to get overwhelmed about the future, I stop myself and head in a different direction. I live each day as fully as I can. I'm fortunate to live near the ocean and some wonderful outdoor scenery, including many nice city and state parks.

I'm adding more visits to the outdoors to experience nature's beauty and serenity more frequently.

"Recovering from loss takes more than time. It takes choices," said Elizabeth Harper Neeld in her wonderful book, *Seven Choices*. I plan to make the most of the rest of my life, but I'm also realistic about what I should do next, including preparing for my death. I understand that it's not that unusual to think a lot about death after a major loss. It seems like you become more aware of the reality of death and what it means. I'm hoping it will be a constant reminder that I need to continue to live my life fully. I have a general idea of where I want my assets to go. But I really couldn't think much about that the first year after Mac died. Now in the second year, I'm kind of working backward, starting with my simple funeral. I've set aside some money for my final arrangements and instructions on what I would like done. I am fortunate to have a close friend here who is willing to carry out my instructions. At the end of the second year, I was ready to get my will revised with more details written out. It took that much time.

CHAPTER 11.

Guilt

"Love is patient, love is kind. It does not envy, it does not boast, it is not proud...Love does not delight in evil but rejoices with the truth. It always protects, always trusts, always hopes, always perseveres." —1 Corinthians 13 (NIV)

I had a hard time crying immediately after Mac died, but in the aftermath, the tears came privately and often. At first, I thought there must be something wrong with me. I've learned to accept that God had his way of helping me cope with the loss, although it took almost two years to totally come to that conclusion. Since Mac died, I have struggled with bouts of feeling guilty for not being more involved in his health issues during our relationship. I understand that type of guilt is normal. Because Mac had a long-term illness of heart disease, we learned to live with his ever-present pain and suffering. While I always knew he could die at any time, we lived life as if he would always be there. Yes, we made changes. But we didn't want to entertain the idea that we should drastically adjust our lifestyle. I wanted him to have hope to keep him alive, and we lived as normal of a life as possible.

One regret that remains is that we decided not to attend the Sigma Delta Chi Chapter of the Society of Professional Journalists award ceremony in

2010 during which Mac was to be recognized at the national level. He was new at his job in Daytona Beach, and we were short on money. We should have gone. Events like this I now recognize are very important. It was not until the second year that I learned to forgive myself for not doing more of those important things. I have come to appreciate that this guilt was not helping me make changes in my own life, and that it was an obstacle to my personal growth. While I never believed God was punishing me, I did believe that He could help me address the issue.

One book I read about the mourning process was *Seven Choices: Finding Daylight after Loss Shatters your World* by Elizabeth Harper Neeld. She quoted Dr. Beverley Raphael as saying memories of the relationship are sifted through at one early phase of the grief process, "studying and investigating thoroughly." Much of the process must be done in solitude and quietness, Neeld concluded. I found that provided a good explanation of how the mind works, and it explained why the solitude time was important. One thing the mourning process has taught me is patience. While at times in my life I have had a lot of patience, I have come to appreciate, since Mac's death, the power of waiting for answers, even on little things.

I honestly never thought seriously about dating the first year. I was too busy responding to "fires" and surviving with a new way of life. It wasn't until the second half of the second year I started to ponder the idea. I've continued to have male friends who were just that, and we thought the same way. I'm still in no hurry now that I'm closer to the end of the second year. I was never in a hurry prior to dating Mac either, and it worked out fine. Ironically, one of my friends in the early months after Mac died was someone who knew me when I was single, prior to marrying Mac. He also knew Mac. It has turned out to be an invaluable friendship because he knew both of us, even though it has entirely been through emails. I'm all for technology. I don't shy away from it at all. But finding "dates" online? I'm still not sure.

Everything I read suggests widows are different than divorcees and other single people. Widows—especially older widows—have concerns other single people may not have. They are warned they may be perceived as caregivers, looked at for financial security or simply seen as someone to fill loneliness. Whatever I decide, I want to go about it slowly—enjoying people and getting to know them first. I guess in some ways I have an advantage. I'm comfortable being single, and I also know the importance and pure joy of having good friends. I think it will be like a lot of things I see in life—an adventure that's worth exploring. Living in Florida, there is no lack of widowers or widows for that matter.

CHAPTER 12.

Returning Home—and to Other Things Familiar

"...let us think of the great family of the heavy-hearted into which our grief has given us entrance, and inevitably, we will feel about us their arms, their sympathy, their understanding." —Helen Keller, *Peace at Eventide*

It's possible for me to avoid driving by the home where Mac had his heart attack in 2013. (I live nearby but go to work in a different direction.) There are occasions when I do return to see the neighbors, especially to see a couple who helped me in the months after Mac died. I did visit them during the 2014 holiday season to deliver a gift. Near the house is a small pond where a group of wood storks call home. Mac and I affectionately called the birds "old men" because of the way their bodies looked hunched over. I had to smile that the storks' numbers were still high a year after Mac's death, even though traditionally they were more comfortable farther south toward the Everglades.

It was in that modest neighborhood in central Florida that I learned the importance of asking people for help, and the neighborhood was very gracious. I never had a victim mentality after Mac's death. In fact, I struggled with just the opposite—I thought I could do it all on my own. I didn't even personally know the neighbors at the time of Mac's death; we met when I was selling Mac's barely running car. We've remained friends until this day.

I agree one should not compare the severity of the death with other types of death. The severity depends on the person involved. But as my friend Ann likes to remind me, Mac took care of me—from how he died (in bed as he awoke for the morning), to how everything seemed to fall in place that first year, one step at a time. I'd like to think God had a part, too. Mac's immediate death gave me the freedom to concentrate on a new life, even though it was not the life I had planned to live. I was left with a modest life insurance policy and a ton of debt, including a house in Alabama that was underwater. In addition, we had just signed a year lease on the house I now lived in and knew I couldn't afford for the long run. Riding out the lease ended up being a blessing. I always liked a line from author Anne Morrow Lindbergh: "For happiness one needs security, but joy can spring like a flower even from the cliffs of despair."

It was being in that predicament where I learned the value of downsizing—that we really need very little to survive and be happy, and that decluttering does open your mind to so much more. That neighborhood in Port Orange in the end brought much joy, even though I didn't like it all that much when Mac was alive. By the time I left, I pretty much liked everyone because they had been so kind.

Other places Mac and I lived I'll visit when the time seems appropriate. I plan to visit Paducah, Kentucky, where Mac was an editorial page editor, and I was a reporter for more than eight years. We lived in an old 1860s house in Lovelaceville that I will never forget. It was there that Mac recovered from his mechanical heart valve surgery in late 1999 and early 2000.

As the years pass, the experience of Mac's death has left me with a new way of looking at the places and the people who had been a part of my life. I rarely see things in black and white anymore—I see the people in my life and the events more openly and with more compassion. And in some cases, the places "we" loved have turned into memories, but not places I will revisit.

I eventually started to learn how to help others who were grieving. Sometimes when you are living through the loss of a loved one, you forget just how far you have come, and then the focus starts to shift to others. I remember how important it was to me at first to have people around who had lost loved ones. I now hope that people who are grieving will look to me as someone who has some understanding of what they are going through. One thing I've learned from mourning is that I've become more empathetic, and that the immediate response to a new widow is to be there for her silently listening, hugging and crying as the need arises.

About a year after Mac died, a friend and fellow Guardian ad Litem (GAL) volunteer lost her husband from a sudden heart attack. I wanted to be there for her. She felt comfortable enough to talk about her loss. We had met during the GAL training process, and I liked her immediately. While her circumstances were different than mine, we shared having a spouse die suddenly. I especially liked meeting with her for lunch prior to going to a training session for the GAL program to see how she was progressing and to "compare notes." I learned the value of listening while being with Mary.

I've decided I'd like to give other widows copies of *Healing After Loss* by Martha W. Hickman. I received a lot of comfort reading the book. My GAL pal was the first person to whom I gave a copy of the book. I also plan to keep a copy of the book on hand. Loss of a close loved one gives you a better understanding of those going through loss even when you don't know them well. I think it just makes you a better, more caring, person overall.

A student I see at the college where I work tragically lost her son. I felt so much compassion for her and wanted to help. I think people who have lost someone close to them want to give back. I truly believe, as the Bible says, that God measures everyone by how they treat widows. As is said in 2 Corinthians, "the Father of compassion and the God of all comfort, who comforts us in all our troubles, so that we can comfort those in any trouble with the comfort we ourselves receive from God." (2Corinthians 1:4, NIV)

At my church, Kitty has helped organize a grief group; I always like to see her. It was almost two years after Mac died when I decided to go to church for a Friday night potluck and the movie, *Shadowlands*, a story about one of my favorite authors, C.S. Lewis. Throughout the movie, there were tears in my eyes, and it was Kitty who noticed that my loss was still hard for me. She is a model of compassion, and I hope to follow in her footsteps. Those are some big shoes to fill.

CHAPTER 13.

When It Comes to Retirement

"Trust in the LORD with all your heart, and lean not on your
own understanding; in all your ways acknowledge Him, and
He shall direct your paths." (Proverbs 3:5-6, NKJV)

I see myself imitating the bees that Frances de Sales describes—they do
not leave a flower as long as they can extract honey. If they no longer see
honey after trying it for a while, they proceed calmly on and do not rush.
Even though he was talking about a daily spiritual practice, that's the way I
plan to look at retirement. I don't want to quit working as long as the work
provides "honey." I see myself starting a somewhat new "career" as a result of
Mac's death—or at least a combination career as I enter my pre-retirement
years. Now that I'm in my 60s, I'm interested in integrating my writing background with my teaching background, something that I have always wanted
to do. It seems that I see that more clearly now and am more motivated to
make it happen.

While I'm not interested in becoming a full-time journalist again, I have
always enjoyed the challenge of writing and seeing what I can do with that

skill. Mac should have written a book, but he never had the time. In some ways, I see Mac guiding me through this book in place of the book he never wrote. While I'm not the type of writer he was, I do believe he offers me the encouragement to better myself as a writer.

I also enjoy education, especially at the community college level in Florida where I have worked since 2011. I love to see those students succeed. I get so much out of my current job; almost every day is rewarding because as a learning specialist, I am able to help people in such an individual way. That is important to me.

Another aspect of my current job that I love is that I am continually learning new things. For example, I have to keep up with technology. I have access to so much knowledge with a library readily available. It's the kind of knowledge I would probably seek if I were retired, but I am now doing it as part of my job. How lucky is that? I've also learned so much from the students; they inspire me. Many of them have overcome so much more than I have, and with far fewer resources, and they seem to keep it together.

For example, one student named Deb, struggled through one math class three times, but she never gave up. When she passed her final math class and graduated, she shared that experience with me. It was awesome.

I especially like the idea of encouraging and showing compassion to people each day. Mac's death—and the grieving process—has made me more empathetic. I can relate better to people who share their concerns with me. I've come to believe that I want to continue working as long as the job I am doing is helping others while I'm having fun.

Widows can start collecting a lesser amount of Social Security at age sixty, but I opted not to collect Social Security because I can still earn more than Social Security pays. More importantly, I don't need to work, but I want to work. I have worked all my life, and I don't see myself staying at home. Mac's death—and being laid off four months later—offered me the chance to look at a variety of new possibilities. While it was scary, it was also an adventure— exploring all kinds of ideas for work and retirement.

I really wanted to experience grief with the hope that the future feelings of joy would be as intense as the joy I've had most of my life. I did have—and still do—a lot of hope for the future. I think of hope as described in Hebrews in the Bible as "an anchor for the soul, firm and secure." (Hebrews 6:19, NIV)

But even with hope firmly intact, during the second year there were times when the reality of my situation would hit like a sudden downpour during a Florida summer. The death of a spouse very much brings home the reality that you no longer have someone in your household to watch over you. I've been blessed with pretty good health and a strong will. Both have helped me as a widow. So the importance of keeping up with routine health procedures became paramount.

Friends are great, but it's not quite the same when you walk in a doctor's office and a spouse is there to support you. That's another adjustment I've made in my new life. I did not gain weight the first year after Mac died; in fact, I lost weight, in part, because of long walks on the beach. But, boy, did I gain the second year, and it was very uncomfortable. It seemed as I was feeling more and more comfortable with the loss of Mac, the more weight I gained and the less I exercised. I was happy just to read and write, but I knew I had to start moving. I began transitioning to a new plan for exercising and eating healthier. And my new mantra became "Take Care of Yourself."

I also, oddly, started drinking more the second year. I had always been one who enjoyed a glass of wine with friends. During the last few years with Mac, however, we drank very little because he simply couldn't drink that much with all his medications. After Mac died, I would often include a glass of wine while socializing. But, somewhere during that second year, I started drinking a glass—or two—in the evening after work, alone in my apartment. I started to realize my drinking may be a problem when I would use coupons for $15 off a $100 wine purchase. And while I did give away a few bottles here and there, I was mostly drinking that wine at home. I eventually made a deal with myself. When I moved to a new apartment, I would see if I could also go back to the old days of not drinking alone, but only drinking socially. I'm happy to say that adjustment was easier than I thought it would be, but it was also a reminder of how easy it is to fall into bad habits as a widow.

As I craft my life now, I recognize it would be nice to spend more time with my retired friends, but I'm hoping to work that in along the way. Whatever I end up doing, I want to volunteer more. A verse in the book of Romans especially hit home: "Do not conform to the pattern of this world but be transformed by the renewing of your mind. Then you will be able to test and approve what God's will is—his good, pleasing and perfect will." (Romans 12:2, NIV)

In one book I read during the mourning process, *Seven Choices*, the author quoted Peter Marris saying, "a widow has to give up her husband without giving up all that he meant to her..." And that's what my future holds. In giving up Mac, I have added a more in-depth reliance on God. It reminds me of God's promise to Joshua in the Old Testament: "Be strong and of good courage, do not fear nor be afraid of them; for the LORD your God, He *is* the One who goes with you. He will not leave you nor forsake you." (Deuteronomy 31:6, NKJV)

CHAPTER 14.

Final Note

"And this is my prayer: that your love may abound more and more in knowledge and depth of insight, so that you may be able to discern what is best and may be pure and blameless for the day of Christ, filled with the fruit of righteousness that comes through Jesus Christ—to the glory and praise of God." (Philippians 1:1, NIV)

The night before Mac died on Thanksgiving Day 2013, we laughed our way through the movie, *Trains, Planes and Automobiles*, playing on TV. Now, two years later, I sit in an apartment watching the same movie. It's about the only part of two years ago that is remotely the same.

This year as part of the long Thanksgiving weekend, I am with my sister, her three children, and a month-old grand-nephew. A new life has begun. As I finish the second year without Mac, my world continues to be challenging but exciting. I've settled in with a challenging job, a church where I'm accepted, a community where I'm comfortable, and friends I love. And the changes continue.

Like so many things in life, the ultimate intent of writing this book wasn't what I expected—it has probably helped me more than anyone else. My ultimate intent is, however, that I've offered at least a little hope for other widows. When I was a graduate student at Louisiana State University in Baton Rouge, the locals would often use the word *lagniappe*, meaning something extra given at no cost. It's a word that I have always loved, and I hope you sensed *lagniappe* while reading this book.

I also hope to continue to share my reflections on being a widow. Look for a website, blog, and maybe a podcast in places I never thought I would go. As for the future, I end with this quote from *Moby Dick* by Herman Melville: "God keep me from ever completing anything." I hope my desire to help widows never ends.

ADDENDUM
Thanksgiving 2015

Dear Mac,

It has been two years since your sudden death from a heart attack at our home in Florida. I'm sorry we will never be able to share old age together. But we had known for most of our twenty-two years of marriage that it was always a possibility. I guess we never thought you would outlive me, now that I think about it.

What I miss most about you were our conversations. Everyone knew you for your intelligence. I knew that, too, but I also knew you as a vociferous reader and learner. I learned so much from you. I hope some of it has rubbed off.

Thank you for the richness you have brought my life. And thank you for showing me a part of you that you never showed anyone else. I saw a gentle soul who was always hard on himself. I will always remember how hard a worker you were and how much you cared about getting it right. That's why you made such a great journalist.

And I will always remember how much you loved me and would come to me with the good and bad. I would be the first person you called when you found out you received yet another award. And when there was bad medical or car news, you would call as soon as you were told.

I remember the year you died—the year you turned sixty; you turned to me and said, "Not bad for sixty." I knew you were proud with how far you had come under trying health conditions. And it was still important to turn to me for my opinion.

On the day before your heart attack, I'll always remember you telling me about your $1,300 car repair. And I'm so glad I reassured you that I would use my Christmas bonus that year to pay for it.

It's hard now to enjoy the days we enjoyed. You never missed a birthday, anniversary, Valentine's Day, or Christmas. I plan to reread the Valentine and anniversary cards. I have saved them all.

I'd like to ask you to forgive me for anything as a wife you think I didn't fulfill. And I forgive you for anything as a husband you didn't fulfill. I believe you had already died by the time I was able to get to you from the next room, but I can only hope that you were aware of how hard I tried to keep you alive, and how I responded immediately to your scream.

Because you died just before you would normally awake, every morning when I awake now, I thank God I am alive. I will do that forever.

I love you. I wished I had said "I love you" more often, even though that was common. I now say "I love you" on all "our days" we enjoyed together. I'm keeping your memories alive in small, but precious ways. I hope to do more "formal memories" as money and time allows.

I have found ways to integrate your memories into what I have become, including many of the valuable lessons that I learned from you. I find many of your values have helped me to redefine my values. It also keeps your memory and honor alive.

I want to thank you for your love and friendship. And I want to thank you for my new way of looking at the beauty and importance of life. I can't help but think you have a say in that and that you are looking out for me. And I am so grateful that I chose you to love and that you chose me. Our lives have been so enriched as a result, especially mine. My world would have been so limited without you. And as time passes, I find my memories of you growing deeper with an understanding of all that you brought to our relationship.

Goodbye. I love you.

Anne

Anne Thrower